Useful Knots

Geoffrey Budworth

THE LYONS PRESS
Guilford, Connecticut
An imprint of The Globe Pequot Press

First Lyons Press edition 2005

The Lyons Press is an imprint of The Globe
Pequot Press.

Originally published in 2004 by Hamlyn, a
division of Octopus Publishing Group Ltd.,
London

Printed and bound in China

10 9 8 7 6 5 4 3 2 1

ISBN 1-59228-602-X

Library of Congress Cataloging-in-Publication
Data is available on file.

contents

Directory of knots

The solid circle shows the best or most popular use of each knot.
The coloured bands indicate the "top ten" most useful knots.

KNOT	PAGE	⛵	🐾	🐦	🏠	DESCRIPTION
KNOTS: stoppers, bindings and shortenings						
Double overhand knot	12	○	○	○	●	Stopper knot for cord, string and twine
Figure-of-eight knot	13	●	○	○	○	Stopper knot for sheets, halyards, etc.
Ashley's stopper knot	14	●	○	○	○	Bulky stopper knot for all occasions
Reef knot (square knot)	15	○	○	○	●	Binding knot for parcels, bandages, etc.
Strangle knot	16	○	○	○	●	Useful bag knot
Pole hitch	17	○	○	○	●	Lashing for long poles, etc.
Constrictor knot	18	○	○	○	●	Best all-round binding knot
Double constrictor knot	20	●	○	○	○	Reinforced binding knot
BENDS: joining knots						
Tape knot	22	○	●	○	○	Recommended for tape or webbing
Sheet bend	24	○	○	○	●	Traditional join for lines of slightly different size
Albright knot	26	○	○	●	○	Joins different-sized monfilaments
Fisherman's knot	27	○	○	○	●	Strongest method of joining fine lines
Double and triple fisherman's knot	28	○	●	○	○	Reinforced method of joining fine lines
Figure-of-eight bend	30	○	●	○	○	Strong and secure joining knot
Zeppelin bend	31	●	○	○	○	Strong undo-able bend for the heaviest shock loads
Vice versa	32	●	○	○	○	Interwoven bend for slippery or wet lines
Carrick bend	33	●	○	○	○	Strong join for larger ropes and cables
Blood knot	34	○	○	●	○	Joins fine lines of almost similar size
Plaited or braided splice	36	○	○	●	○	Stong shock-absorbing joining knot
HITCHES: taking the load						
Knute hitch	40	○	○	○	●	Attaches a line to anything with an aperture
Buntline hitch	41	●	○	○	○	Attaches a line securely to a ring, eye, etc.
Ground-line hitch	42	●	○	○	○	Simple hitch to rope or rail
Pedigree cow hitch	43	○	○	○	●	Quick, simple hitch to post or rail
Cow hitch variation	44	○	○	○	●	Attachment to post or rail

KNOT	PAGE	⛵	🧗	🎣	🏠	DESCRIPTION
hitches continued						
Clove hitch	45	●	○	○	○	Simple, all-purpose hitch
Round turn & two half-hitches	46	○	○	○	●	Dependable hitch to post or rail
Timber & killick hitches	47	○	○	○	●	Quick hitch to drag or tow a load
Camel hitch	48	●	○	○	○	Secure hitch for wet lines
Boom hitch	49	●	○	○	○	Extra secure hitch to spar or rail
Lighterman's hitch	50	●	○	○	○	Towing or mooring hitch, guy-line attachment
Pile hitch	52	●	○	○	○	Versatile knot for end or bight attachment to post
World's fair knot	53	○	○	●	○	Attaches mono to hook, lure or swivel
Palomar knot	54	○	○	●	○	Attaches most lines to hooks, lures, swivels or arbors. Good for braided lines
Jansik special	55	○	○	●	○	Strong knot for attaching hooks, lures or swivels
Trilene knot	56	○	○	●	○	Attaches lines to hooks or swivels with eyes
Domhof knot	57	○	○	●	○	Attaches lines to hooks or swivels with straight ends
Prusik knot	58	○	●	○	○	Classic slide-and-grip knot
Extended French prusik knot	60	○	●	○	○	Innovative prusik knot for tape
Cat's paw	62	○	○	○	●	Secure attachment to hook or rail

LOOPS: sliding and fixed circular loops

KNOT	PAGE	⛵	🧗	🎣	🏠	DESCRIPTION
Double overhand loop knot	64	○	○	●	○	Strong loop for tackle rig
Triple overhand loop knot	65	○	○	●	○	Very strong loop for tackle rig
Scaffold knot	66	●	○	○	○	Versatile adjustable loop
Bowline in the bight	67	●	○	○	○	Forms a double loop in the middle of a line
Bowline	68	●	○	○	○	General purpose, single fixed loop
Triple bowline and variation	70	○	●	○	○	Creates a sit sling, chest sling or full harness
Angler's loop knot	72	○	○	●	○	Fixed loop to attach to just about anything
Alpine butterfly	74	○	●	○	○	Creates a loop in the middle of a line
Frost knot	76	○	●	○	○	Makes tape or webbing stirrups (étriers)
Midshipman's hitch	78	●	○	○	○	Slide-to-lock adjustable loop
Tarbuck knot	79	○	○	○	●	General purpose slide-and-grip knot
Figure eight loops	80	○	●	○	○	Reliable alternative to the common bowline
Rapala knot	84	○	○	●	○	Small fixed loop for plugs and lures
Blood knot loop	86	○	○	●	○	Joins lines of almost similar sizes
Bimini twist	88	○	○	●	○	Strongest loop for big-game fishing
Plaited or braided loop	90	○	○	●	○	Strong, shock-absorbing fixed loop
Adjustable loop and bend	92	○	●	○	○	Slide-and-grip shock-absorbing bend

Terms, tips and techniques

Types of rope

Rope, cord, string and twines were once all made from the shredded and combed fibres of plant stems, stalks and leaves. Cotton, coir, sisal, manilla and hemp were the renewable and eco-friendly crops from which vegetable-fibre ropes were made. They could be hard on the hands and all the cordage was, by today's standards, weak and cumbersome. Natural-fibre rope was somewhat stronger when wet (as are synthetics) but then it tended to rot.

Natural-fibre ropes have been replaced almost entirely by modern synthetics. Nylon is marketed under trade names such as Polyamid, Bri-nylon and Enkalon. Polyester appears as Terylene, Dacron, Tergal and Fortrel. The expensive organic polymer aramid is sold as Kevlar. Then there is cheaper polypropylene. Newer products include Dyneema, Spectra and Admiral 2000. A competent supplier will sort out what you need, but basically nylon stretches and so is suitable for anchor warps or tow lines where some give is crucial, whereas Terylene does not and is used for standing rigging and in any other case where stretch is unwanted. Kevlar has a remarkable strength-to-weight ratio and can replace wire rigging, but it can be easily damaged by abrasion and must be sheathed in tough polyester. Weaker, lighter cordage (e.g. polypropylene) may float and make a useful heaving line. Man-made cordage comes in many colours, so it is now usual to colour-code yacht halyards and sheets, or merely to follow fashion in rigging a sail-board or canoe.

The problem with man-made fibre ropes, spun from monofilaments, is that they are smooth and slippery, with less grip, and trusted knots may perform badly in them. The usual advice is to add a half-hitch or two for extra security; the long-term answer may be to come up with more suitable knots. Some manufacturers chop their long monofilaments into shorter staple lengths, which recreates the hairy surface texture of rope originally made from leaves and stalks and roots of plants.

Rope sizes

Older knot books refer to rope size by circumference in inches. Today, all cordage is known by its diameter in centimetres (or millimetres). Rope is traditionally anything with over a 1-in circumference (10-mm diameter). Ropes for special purposes are referred to as lines (bowline, stern line, tow line, clothes-line). Smaller stuff, as it is informally called, is cordage or (if thinner still) string or twine.

Strength and security

Strength and security are different characteristics in a knot. Relative knot strength – or efficiency – is the breaking strength of a knotted rope, compared with the same rope unknotted. The overhand knot, for example, has a strength of about 45 per cent; in other words, it more than halves the breaking strength of any line in which it is allowed to remain, so it should not be used for anything vital. A steady pull is not the same as putting a shock loading on a knotted rope (e.g., when a climber falls and is brought up short). Then the momentum equals the mass multiplied by its speed and direction. To withstand such stresses and strains, the rope should be tied with one or other of the slide-and-grip friction knots, which are designed to absorb energy and ensure that the knot does not capsize and break the line.

Knots, bends and hitches

A knot is the generic name for any loop or entanglement of flexible material, created either intentionally or accidentally, by a tucked end or bight. The word also has a very precise meaning:

A knot, as distinct from a bend or hitch (see below), secures two ends of the same material, e.g., a bandage, parcel string or shoelace. In addition, a knot is anything (including a bend or hitch) tied in small stuff – thus all anglers' knots are by definition merely knots, irrespective of form or function.

A bend is a knot that joins two separate ropes or bits of cordage together.

A hitch attaches a line to a rail, post, ring or perhaps to another rope (or even onto itself).

There is often more than one way to tie complex knots and knot enthusiasts bore and bewilder if they insist on showing them all. This book illustrates one quick and easy way to learn and use each knot, only showing alternative methods where these are needed to cope with different circumstances.

Other useful terms

The end of a line used to tie knots is referred to as the working end or (by anglers) the tag end or (if it is being pulled out of your hand) the bitter end. The other is the standing end. In-between is the standing part. When this portion of the line is doubled it is called a bight, until it is crossed over itself and becomes a loop, maybe with an elbow.

Wrapping a rope around a post or rail, to take the strain of a moving boat or a heavy load, is called 'taking a turn', but bringing the working end around an extra half a turn, prior to making fast, creates a round turn.

A simple knot with something through it is a half-hitch. Finish off a round turn with two half-hitches rather than two reversed half-hitches.

Stopper knots

To minimize waste from fraying, you may tie an overhand knot in the end. The overhand knot needs no explanation – we can all do it – except to reiterate that it reduces the breaking strength of rope or cordage to a mere 45 per cent of the unknotted line. If the working end is not pulled completely through, leaving a draw-loop (see below), a somewhat stronger (45–50 per cent) stopper knot is made, which can be used to restring musical instruments. To secure something bulkier, tie an overhand knot in the bight.

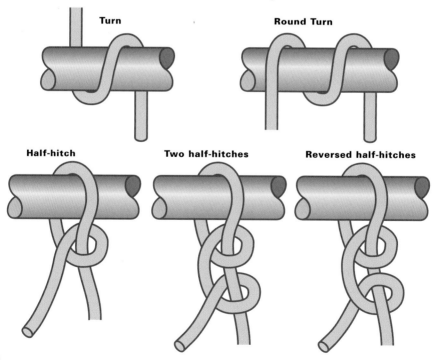

Turn **Round Turn**

Half-hitch **Two half-hitches** **Reversed half-hitches**

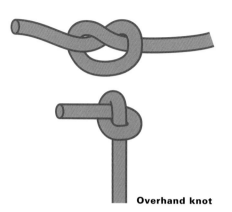

Overhand knot

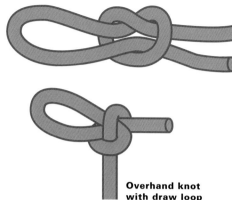

**Overhand knot
with draw loop**

To prevent jib leads, main halyards, flag halyards, etc., coming unreeved from blocks, fairleads or other slots or holes, use a figure eight knot (4–5). This knot appears to have been named by Darcy Lever in his book *Sheet Anchor* (1908). With or without a draw-loop, it is more easily undone than an overhand knot, and with one it may be slightly stronger (45–50 per cent). Do not leave it flat but pull the standing part so that the working end is pulled over and trapped beneath the bight. Although bulkier than the overhand knot, it does not have a larger diameter. It will pull out of the same size hole as the overhand knot. If you need to use something bigger, choose Ashley's stopper knot (see p. 14).

Draw-loops

When the working end is not pulled completely through the knot, a draw-loop is created. Tug on that end and it acts as a quick-release to undo the knot. Some knots, such as the common

bowline, may actually be strengthened by the extra rope part within the body of the knot. Such knots are also less likely to jam. So, unless you want a semi-permanent knot, draw-loops should be used wherever possible. Note that if you treat both working ends of a reef knot (see p. 15) as draw-loops, you will end up with the familiar double reef bow used to tie shoelaces.

Multiple overhand knots

This technique must be learned by all who tie knots – especially by anglers

**Overhand knot
in the bight**

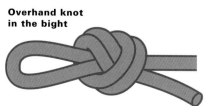

and climbers. They are also known as blood knots (from their past use by surgeons) or barrel knots (because of their shape). Tie an overhand knot, then tuck the working end a second time, for a double overhand knot (see p. 12). Begin to tighten the knot by pulling gently on both ends – feel how the knot wants to twist and wrap around itself. Allow it to do so, turning the left-hand end up and away from you, and the right-hand one down and towards you. (The instructions given here are for a right-handed knot like that shown in the diagram. They should be reversed for one formed left-handed.) Another tuck creates a triple overhand knot, which requires even more care in shaping the final form.

Fraying

Unfortunately, some types of rope are prone to fraying. Synthetic materials may be heat sealed with care, using a small blow torch or lighter, although heat sealing is not as attractive to the eye as whipping. The latter involves winding thinner cordage around the edge of a rope and burying the ends neatly. Use natural fibres for vegetable fibre ropes and synthetic line for synthetic ropes. Some knots contain elements of whipping to neaten then (see Plaited or braided loop, pp. 90–91).

Using the book

The symbols on the thumb index at the side of every page provides an at-a-glance key that indicates the uses for the knot.

Key to the symbols

 Boating and sailing

 Tips and additional uses

 Caving and climbing

 Cautionary points

 Angling and fishing

 Home and general

knots

The word 'knot' is generally used to refer to any
entanglement of rope or smaller cordage, but
the word also has a narrower meaning that
excludes bends, hitches and loops. The knots
in this section are all either stopper knots or
binding knots.

Knot terminology can be inconsistent,
however – despite their names, the Albright
knot is a bend, the prusik knot is a hitch and
the Tarbuck knot is a loop and they are in the
relevant sections. Conversely, the pole hitch is
actually a binding knot, and so is included in
this section.

'Notice how the ... figure-eight and double overhand knots
change their shape when tightened. Be amenable when a
knot tells you what it wants to do – it usually knows best'

John Shaw, *The Directory of Knots,* **2003**

knots

Double overhand knot

Use: This compact stopper knot may be used on both the smallest-diameter threads or larger cords. It is also the basis of some other knots, including the strangle knot (see p. 16) and bends such as the double fisherman's knot (see p. 28), and should be learned for that reason.

Method: Tie an overhand knot (1) and tuck the working end a second time (2). Pull gently on both ends, and as the knot tightens it will begin to wrap around itself (3). Twist both knot parts, in your fingers, in opposite directions as indicated, to make this happen. Then pull the knot tight (4).

✔ *This knot can be tied in the end of laces or lanyards to prevent ends fraying.*

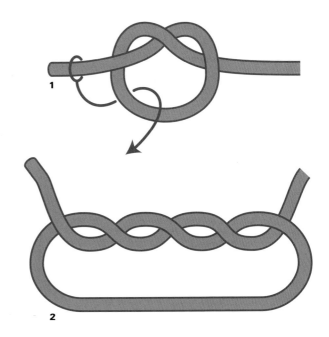

Figure-of-eight knot

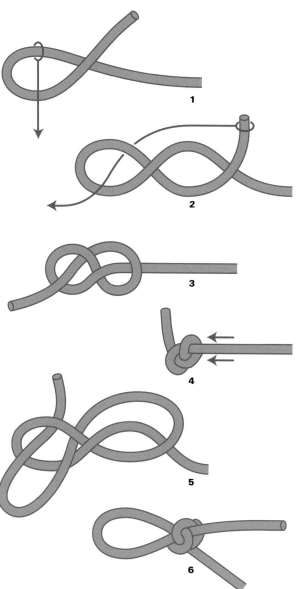

Use: This is a popular stopper knot that is used widely in sailing. It will not block a larger aperture than an overhand knot, but does have the advantage that it can be easily untied after use, whereas the overhand knot is likely to jam.

Method: Form a loop (1) and give it an extra twist. Tuck the end (2) and draw the knot up fairly snug (3) to create the flattish figure-of-eight. Finally, push up against the knot to create the surrounding collar that is characteristic of stopper knots (4). For knots that will not have to endure rough treatment, consider incorporating a draw-loop (5–6).

Tie this knot to the ends of sailboat sheets, halyards and tackles.

Ashley's stopper knot

Use: Use this chunky hole blocker when the figure-of-eight knot is too small.

Method: Tie a simple noose (1–2). Tuck the working end as shown (no other way will do) and pull the noose tight to trap it (3). The completed knot should have a neat trefoil of overlapping parts on its underside.

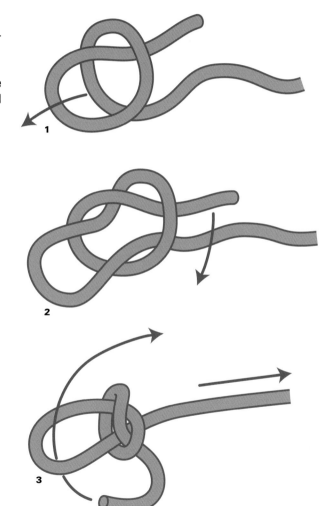

This knot can be used to add a rope handle to a bucket.

Reef knot (square knot)

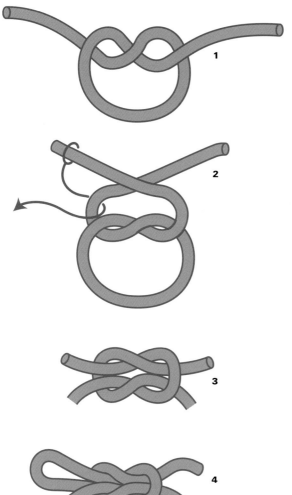

Use: This is a binding knot for tying up parcels of all kinds. On boats it has a variety of uses, including reefing shortened sails with cord reef points, fastening gaskets around furled sails, tying off laced sail covers and fastening down an anchor on deck.

Method: Place one working end on top of the other and tie a half-knot; then place the same end on top of the other again and add a second half-knot (1–2). The working ends must emerge on the same side of the knot. Pull it tight (3). When sailing, a slipped reef knot (4), with a single draw-loop in one end only, is easy to tie.

Good for binding reefed sails, parcels, shoe laces and bandages.

Never use this bend to join working ropes.

15

Strangle knot

Use: This is a general-purpose binding knot. (See also constrictor knot, pp. 18–19.)

Method: Tie a double overhand knot (see p. 12) and slide it onto the object(s) to be bound (1–3). Alternatively, tie it directly round the objects and leave a draw-loop for quick release.

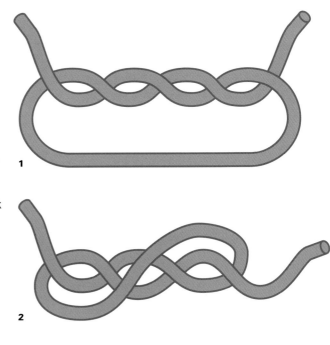

1

2

Good for securing bundles of unwieldy objects.

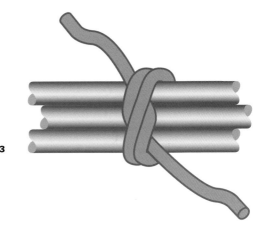

3

Pole hitch

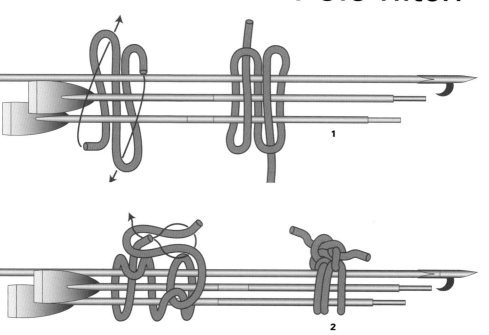

1

2

Use: The pole hitch is a gathering and binding knot. A pair of these will hold assorted long objects.

Method: Arrange the cord in an S- or Z-shape beneath the assembled objects, and tuck both ends through opposite bights (1). Draw tight and tie off with a reef knot (2, and see p. 15).

Great for grouping any awkward armful of objects, from tent poles to garden tools.

Constictor knot

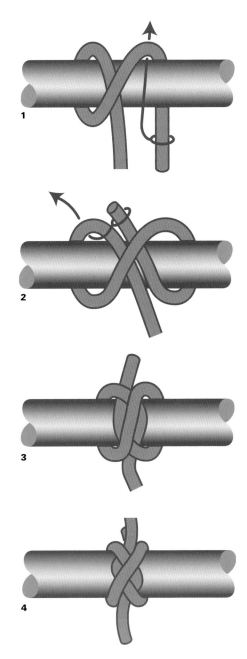

Use: This is the best of all binding knots. Use one or more of them as a temporary whipping on a rope's end, to begin a seizing, as a substitute for hose clamps, to repair a cracked tiller, or to tie a pencil to a clipboard. As a bag or sack knot, tie it with a quick-release draw-loop. It also serves to hold objects being glued together. On soft foundations such as rope, use hard-laid line. For unyielding ones, such as metal rails or rings, use soft and stretchy stuff. Either way the knot will cling and grip like a boa constrictor. There are several different ways in which to tie a constrictor knot.

 Attach tie-on labels or suspend Christmas baubles with this compact knot.

1

2

3

4

18

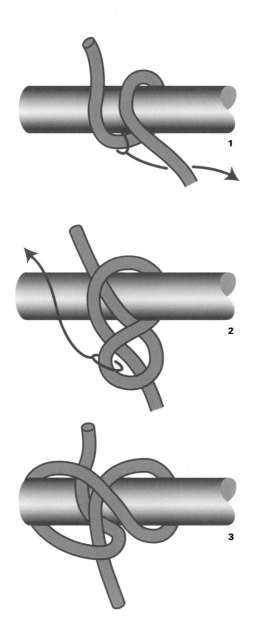

Method 1 – tied with an end Tie a clove hitch (see p. 45) and then knot the two standing parts with a half-knot (1–3). Pull the resulting knot as tight as possible, so that the overlying diagonal strongly reinforces the entwined knot parts (4).

For semi-permanent bindings, tighten the knot by attaching each end of the cord to a fid (or pair of winch handles, screwdrivers, spanners or other robust objects), and pulling them strenuously apart with your hands and feet. If possible, use two opposing cockpit winches. Cut the ends off close to the knot.

Method 2 – tied in the bight It is quicker and easier to tie this knot in the bight, provided the end of whatever is to be bound is accessible. Take a turn (1), pull out a bight and, imparting half a twist (2), pass it over the end of the object (3). Pull tight, as before, and cut the ends off short.

19

Double constrictor knot

Use: Uses include fixing string loops to garden tools so they can be hung up neatly. As the diameter of an object increases, the efficacy of a constrictor knot (see pp. 18–19) is slightly impaired, but this knot rectifies the deficiency.

Method 1 – tied with an end Begin the knot in the usual way, adding a second turn prior to the final tuck (1). Pull tight (2).

Method 2 – tied in the bight First make a clove hitch (1). Swap the upper one of the two ends for the left-hand loop (2), withdraw a bight (3) and, with half a twist, pass it over the end of the object and pull tight (4).

 Tie this when you need an extra secure constrictor knot.

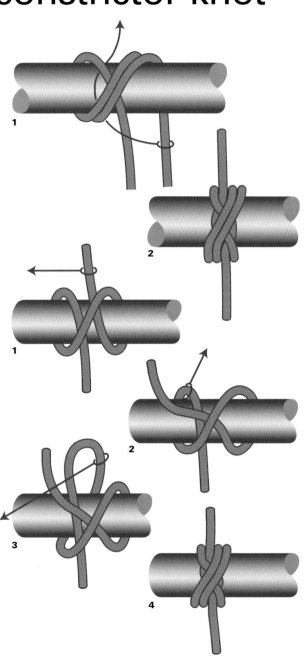

bends

A 'bend' joins two ropes together, whether to give them greater length, allow you to haul into place (or retrieve) a heavy line with a lighter one, or to make fast a mooring rope or painter on a boat to a permanent dock line.

Anglers don't distinguish between knots and bends and use both to join dissimilar materials (fly lines to leaders, leaders to reel lines, monofilament to braid or braid to wire).

'I find great comfort in this knot [the figure-of-eight bend], knowing that it absolutely will not come untied when used to join two rappel ropes'

Duane Raleigh, *Knots & Ropes for Climbers*, **1998**

bends

Tape knot

Use: This is the bend recommended for climbers' tape or webbing. It also works for rope, cord, string and the finest monofilaments. It can be used to form loops (by joining the two ends of a piece of rope) or slings.

1

2

 This is by far the best knot for tying tape.

3

4

Method: In anything up to a couple of metres (6 ft) long, just lay the two lengths parallel and together, then tie an overhand knot (see p. 12) in both at once. Remove unwanted twists in the tape before pulling tight. In longer stuff, tie the overhand knot in the end of one length (1) and pass the other end through and around to mirror the first knot (2). Alternatively, tie both working ends simultaneously (3).

The tape knot is straightforward to tie using webbing, but remember to leave longish working ends, which should then be taped to the adjacent standing parts. Check the knot regularly to make sure it does not work loose. In 25-mm (1-in) tape, at least two 30-cm (1-ft) lengths will be needed for this knot.

When tying a tape knot in rope, you have a choice of two layouts. Both are secure, but one is thought to be weaker than the other. For the strongest knot, the cords must be parallel, with no cross-overs. Then, with the belly of the knot underneath, ensure that both of the short ends emerge on top. If the ends are underneath, the knot may be weakened (4).

23

Sheet bend

Use: The sheet bend is a general-purpose bend for uniting two lines of unequal diameters. It may also be used to attach an end to a loop or small eye. It does, however, have a number of limitations. It will jam under a heavy load and, without an extra tuck, can slip in smooth materials. Security tests have shown it to spill after an average 22 tugs out of 100, and it is not a very strong knot, with a breaking strength of 55 per cent.

Tying up garden plants is best done with this knot, which, if the ends are left long, can then be adjusted to allow for seasonal growth.

Never tie this knot in lines of greatly different diameter or construction, as it may capsize and spill.

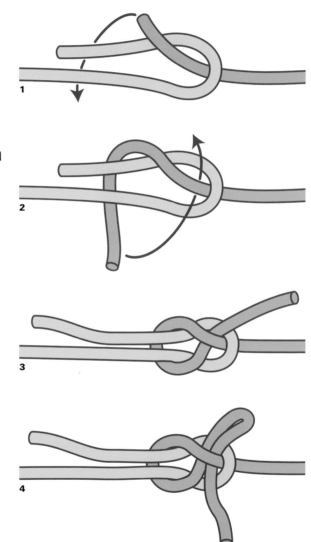

24

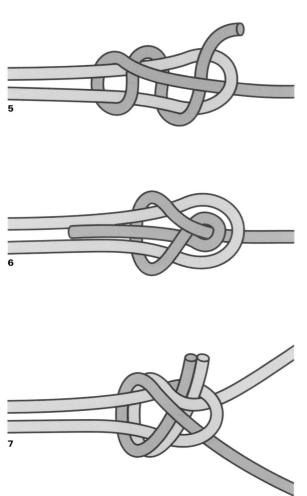

5

6

7

Method: As a general rule, aim to keep both short ends on the same side (1–3). Leave a draw-loop if you prefer (4). For ropes of different size, composition or wetness, use the double sheet bend (5), when the smaller and more flexible cordage makes the double turn around the thicker bight. If the knot is to be subjected to rough treatment, consider reinforcing it with a backward tuck (6), which also makes it more streamlined and easier to pull one way through narrow gaps. Swedish marine writer and artist Frank Rosenow spotted a sheet bend in Greek cruising waters used as a bridle for three converging ropes (7).

Albright knot

Use: This knot joins lines of different size – for example, monofilament to braid or braid to wire.

Method: Make a bight in the thicker of the two lines. Insert and wrap the thinner one around towards the end of the bight (1–2). Finally, tuck the working end (3). Systematically work everything tight (4).

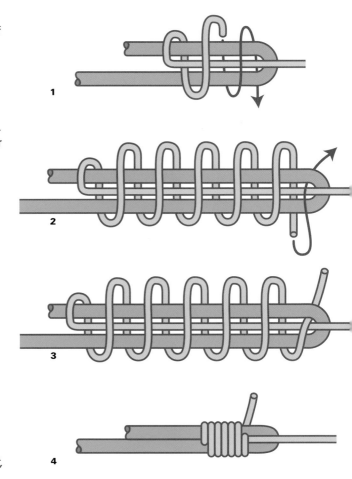

1

2

3

4

Essentially an angling knot, but could be used in cordage, when a sheet bend is not up to the job.

Fisherman's knot

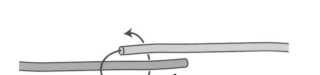

Use: This is a strong and secure bend to join two similar lines.

Method: Lay the two working parts alongside and parallel to one another (1). Tie an identical overhand knot (see p. 12) around each standing part with the other working end (2–3). Pull them together (4–5).

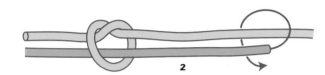

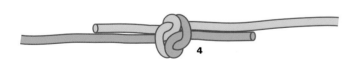

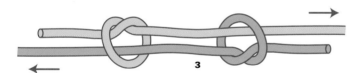

When twine, string or cord will not go far enough join on another length with this knot.

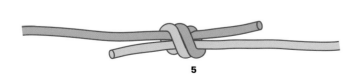

Double and triple fisherman's knot

Use: Use these strengthened knots to secure two ropes together or to make endless slings.

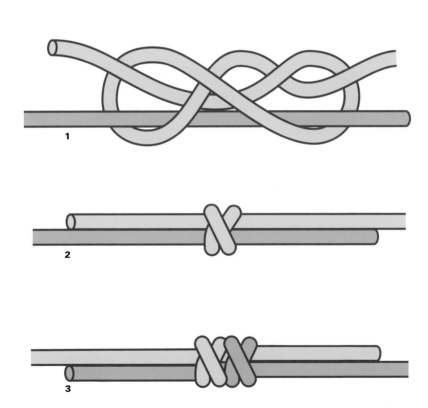

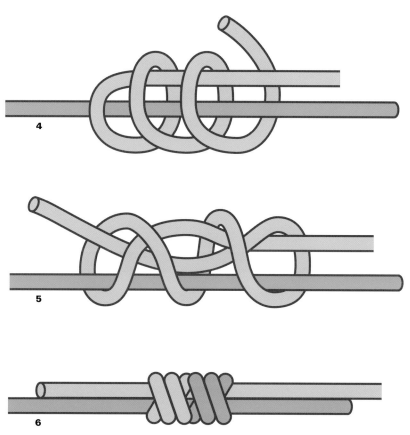

Method: Make two parallel, sliding double overhand knots (1–3, and see p. 12). For slippery cord and conditions, triple overhand knots may be preferred (4–6). Leave generous ends 7–8 cm (3 in) long, and tape them to their adjacent standing parts. The knot will take 75 cm (2½ ft) of 9-mm (³⁄₁₀-in) rope and over 1 metre (3½ ft) of 11-mm (⅖-in) rope.

These knots are for anglers, climbers and rescue workers who depend upon the strongest of knots.

Do not use either of these knots unless you are prepared to cut them off afterwards.

29

Figure-of-eight bend

Use: This is a comparatively strong and secure knot for joining ropes of similar size and construction.

Method: Tie a figure-of-eight in the end of one rope or cord, and then introduce the working end of another line (1). Follow the lead of the original knot exactly as shown (2–3) to double the knot (4). The doubled lead should cross over as it curves, and not resemble parallel train tracks. Work and pull the knot snug, compact and tight (5). The standing part of each line forms the outer bight at each end of the knot. Some climbing authorities say it is stronger that way.

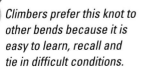

Climbers prefer this knot to other bends because it is easy to learn, recall and tie in difficult conditions.

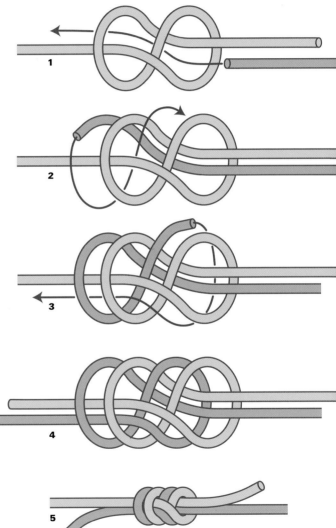

Zeppelin bend

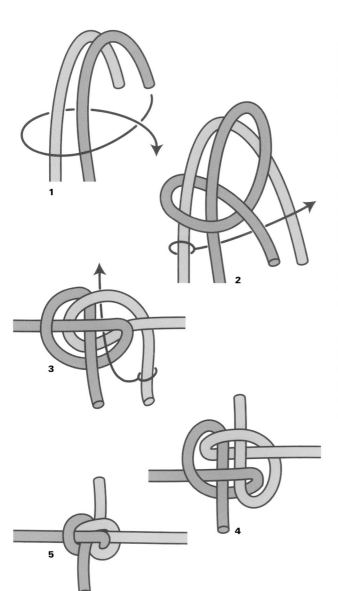

Use: This is probably the best of a whole trustworthy family of symmetrical bends. It works even in big stiff hawsers and cables.

Method: Hold up together the two ends to be joined and let them hang naturally (1). Tie an overhand knot in the foremost one, enclosing the standing part of the other (2). Bring the standing part of the other strand forward and tuck its end up through thr central compartments made by both strands (3, 4). It is secure even with daylight showing through it, but you can pull it snug and fairly tight before use (5).

This is truly ideal for mooring anything that bobs, tugs or jerks about.

Vice versa

Use: Join slimy, slippery or otherwise intractable materials, such as shiny synthetics or shock elastics (bungee cords), with this bend. Craft workers can use this tenacious knot to mend damaged knitting, weaving and needlework.

Method: Marry the two lines, end for end, then tuck, turn and interweave as shown (1–4). Pull it snug and tight (5).

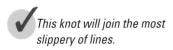

This knot will join the most slippery of lines.

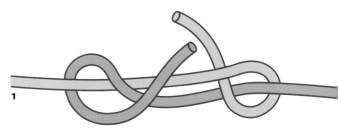

1

2

3

4

5

Carrick bend

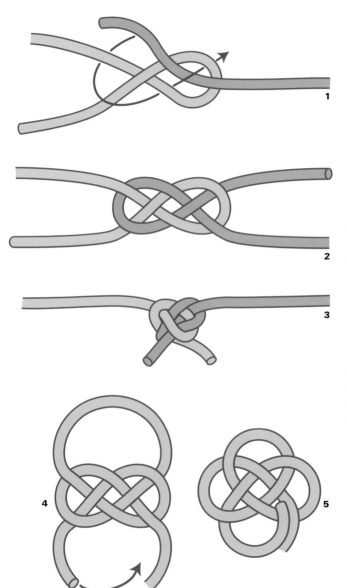

Use: This is a bend for joining larger ropes and cables of the same size and construction.

Method: Weave the ropes over and under, as shown in 1–2. Arrange the layout so that the working ends emerge on opposite sides of the knot. Pull the knot tight, capsizing it into its stable working form (3). The version with both short ends on the same side (4) may be less secure and so is not recommended as a bend. Bring the working end around to re-enter the knot (5), doubling and trebling the lead, to make a decorative Turk's head mat or bracelet.

This knot is sometimes applied by needle workers as a decorative motif to garments and embroidery.

This knot should not be employed to bear a very heavy load.

33

Blood knot

Use: When this knot joins lines of the same size, it has a breaking strength of about 85 per cent. In lines of unequal diameter, the thinner of the two lines must be used double; the knot strength then increases to around 90 per cent.

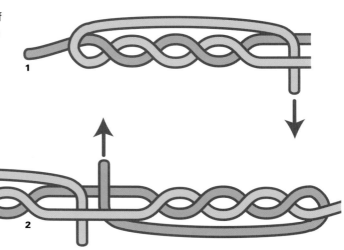

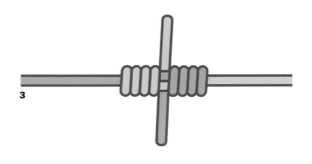

 This knot is specifically for anglers to tie in mono or braided fishing lines.

 It is unsuitable for coarser cordage, as it will not draw up easily, and will be difficult to untie.

Method: Place the lines parallel and together. Wind one working end around the adjacent standing part at least five times, then bring the end back and tuck it between the two standing parts (1). Repeat, going the other way with the other end (2). Pull up snug (3).

Outward-coiled knots must be allowed to wrap around the line as they tighten. On an inward-coiled knot (4–5), the turns are made that way, and so may be preferred.

By doubling up a very thin line, so that it is the same thickness as the one to which it is to be joined, it is possible to make an 'improved' blood knot. In this case, the number of turns in the thinner line should be reduced, otherwise there will be twice as many as in the thicker one, and that is not necessary. (Work out the number of reductions by trial and error.)

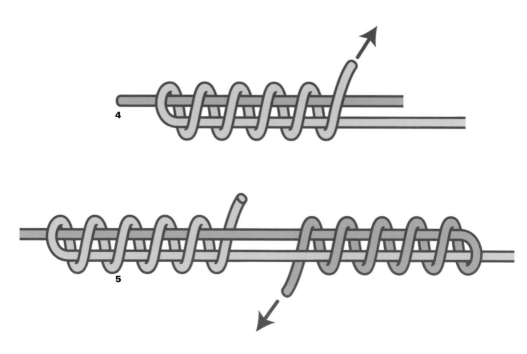

Plaited or braided splice

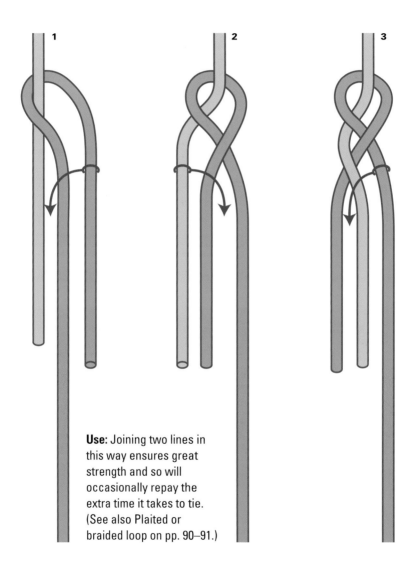

Use: Joining two lines in this way ensures great strength and so will occasionally repay the extra time it takes to tie. (See also Plaited or braided loop on pp. 90–91.)

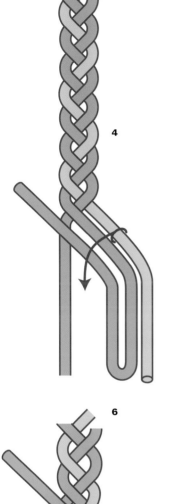

4

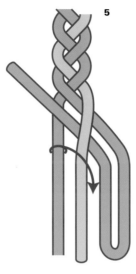

5

Method: Bring together both working ends as shown (1). Bring the right-hand strand across in front of its own standing part to become the centre strand. Then bring the left-hand outer strand over to become the centre strand (2). Now bring the right-hand outer strand over (3); and bring the left-hand outer strand over in a similar way. Repeat this process, then make a bight, using the working end from the strand that formed the initial collar at the start of the plait or braid, and leave a short length of tag end protruding (4).

Continue to plait or braid, treating the doubled bight as a single strand (5–7).

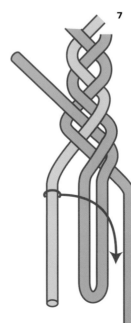

6

7

This knot adds an element of stretch that will absorb sudden shock-loading.

37

When the bight is almost exhausted, tuck the remaining working end down through it (8) and then trap it securely by pulling carefully on the doubled-over strand's tag end (9).

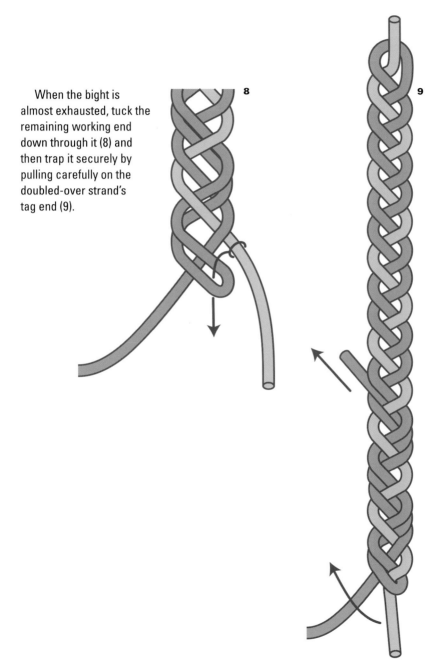

hitches

A hitch attaches a length of line to a hook, ring, post, rail or another rope. Hitches have to withstand the load that will be placed upon them, which may be steady or intermittent, tugging and jerking, occurring at right-angles or length-wise to the anchorage point, or from varying directions. Different hitches suit different conditions. Hitches are usually stronger than loops and bends.

'When horses are tethered they always go to the end of the rope and pull in order to try and reach whatever is furthest away, and so whatever knot is used must be easy to undo even after being pulled on all day'

Ron Edwards, *Knots for Horse-lovers,* **2001**

nitches

Knute hitch

Use: Use the Knute hitch to attach a line to anything with a hole not much larger than twice the diameter of the cordage used. This hitch is often tied to fix lanyards to knives and other tools.

Method: Tie a stopper knot in the working end. Thread a bight through the hole in, for example, a knife handle (1). Trap the working end with it (2). If you prefer you could use a large bead to replace the stopper knot.

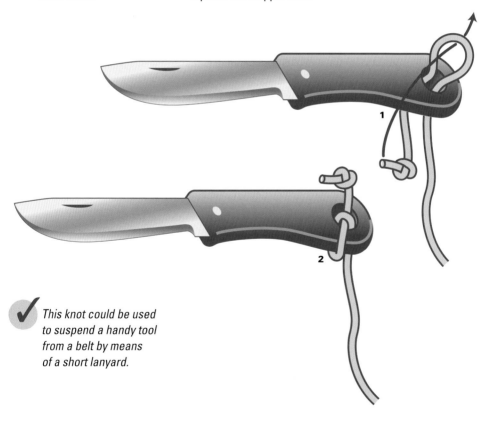

This knot could be used to suspend a handy tool from a belt by means of a short lanyard.

Buntline hitch

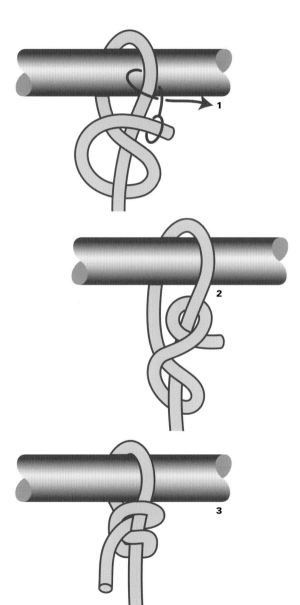

Use: The buntline hitch was traditionally used to secure a lanyard to a cringle, eyelet, ring or swivel. These days it is also used on tools with small holes in their handles. Note the short end trapped on the inside of the knot (3). However, where something more secure than the normal two half-hitches is needed, the buntline hitch is useful. When tied in a strip of material, it turns out to be the common knot used for men's neckties.

Method: Make two half-hitches, tying the second inside the first (1–3).

This knot can be used to make an improvised dog lead by attaching a length of rope to a collar.

Ground-line hitch

Use: This simple but robust hitch is employed by cod fishermen on their trawl nets. If the load is intermittent or varies in direction, it makes a good alternative to a clove hitch.

Method: Begin as if to tie a clove hitch (1, and see p. 45), but vary the final tuck (2). For a quick-release, use a draw-loop (3).

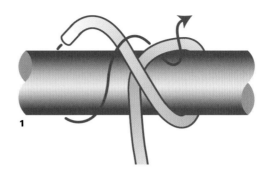

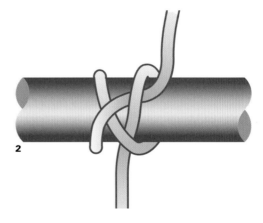

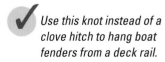 *Use this knot instead of a clove hitch to hang boat fenders from a deck rail.*

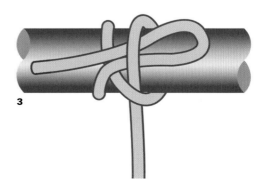

Pedigree cow hitch

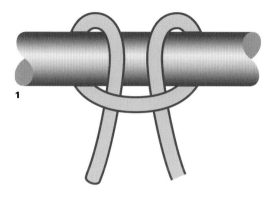

1

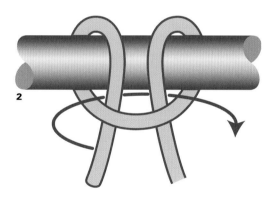

2

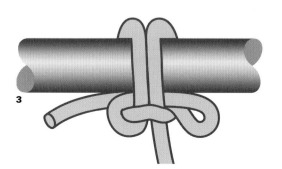

3

Use: This is a quick and simple general-purpose hitch.

Method: The common cow hitch (1) has a working end and a standing part tethered around a rail or post. It is insecure and never to be trusted. To tie this variation, simply tuck and trap the short end through the basic knot (2). In this way, a previously unreliable knot is made fit for honest work. Leave a draw-loop if you prefer (3).

Start roof rack lashings of cordage with this knot.

Cow hitch variation

Use: A stronger version of the common cow hitch, this can be used for all sorts of DIY and craftwork.

Method: After the first half-hitch (1), turn the working end and lead it through the same loop (2). Tighten to a neat finish (3).

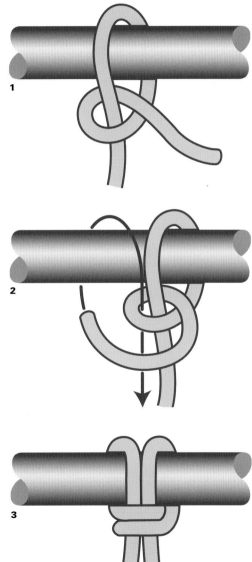

✓ *Attach an outdoor washing line to a convenient post with this hitch.*

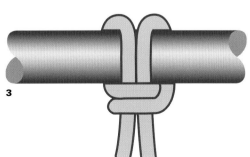

Clove hitch

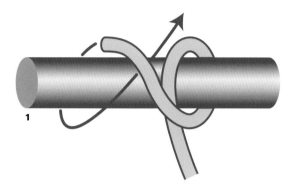

Use: This simple but versatile knot will moor a small boat, suspend a fender or attach any line to a post, rail or ring if the pull is a steady one at right-angles to the point of attachment.

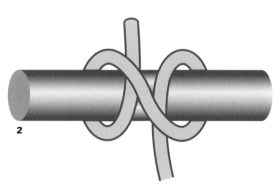

Method: Take a turn around the ring or rail and lay the working end diagonally up and across the standing part (1). Take another turn and tuck the end beneath the diagonal, creating a letter 'N' outline (2). For a temporary task, such as hanging a fender, leave a draw-loop (3).

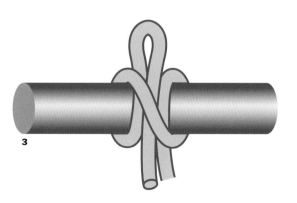

This can provide a quick but temporary mooring knot for small boats.

If the loaded end of a line is tugged about, a clove hitch can work loose, slip and come undone.

45

Round turn & two half-hitches

Use: This is a classic hitch for securing a line to a ring, rail or spar.

Method: Use the friction of the round turn (1) to snub and hold the load; then add the two identical half-hitches (2–3). The two half-hitches have a breaking strength of 60–75 per cent, but the round turn may increase that percentage.

This knot could be used to rig up an improvised washing line.

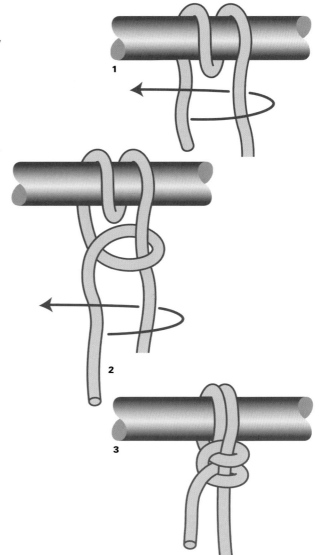

Timber & killick hitches

Use: The timber hitch is a quick and simple knot intended to drag, tow or hoist long objects such as tree trunks and logs, piling and piping. For smoother objects (such as masts or spars), or to give directional stability for a straighter pull, add the half-hitch that turns this knot into a killick hitch. Killick was a naval term for a small anchor.

Method: Make a loop around the intended load, then tie a half-hitch and wrap the working end several times around itself (1) to create a makeshift running eye. This tucking and trapping process is known as 'dogging' the end. Pull the resulting noose tight to make a basic timber hitch. Add another half-hitch some distance from the initial knot to convert it into a killick hitch (2).

Ideal for hauling fallen timber.

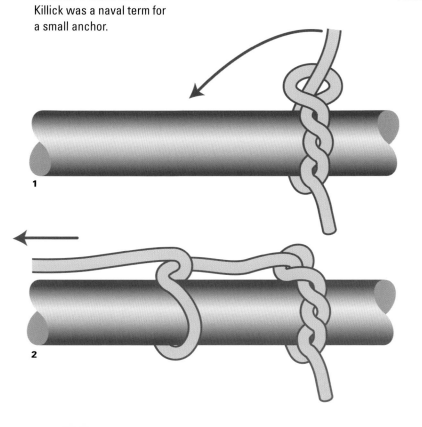

Camel hitch

Use: This hitch attaches a line to mast, spars or rigging in such a way that the pull on it may be from either direction. It also undoes easily wet or dry.

Method: Take a couple of turns around the rope, rail or whatever, and then bring the working end across in front of the standing part and half-hitch it as shown (1). Make a second identical half-hitch, completing a clove hitch (2), and work the completed hitch snug and tight (3).

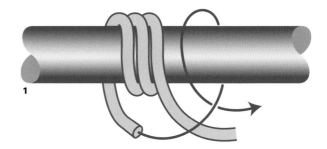

1

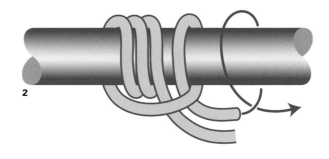

2

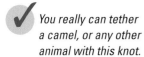 *You really can tether a camel, or any other animal with this knot.*

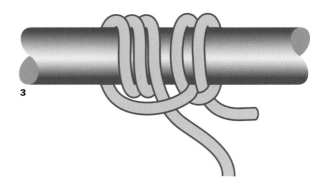

3

Boom hitch

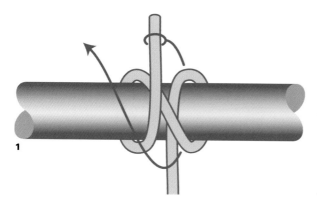

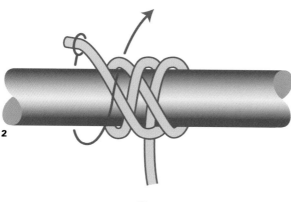

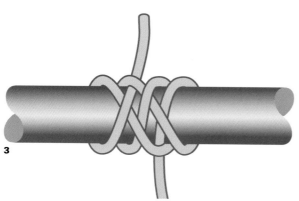

Use: When a clove hitch, ground-line hitch or even a camel hitch is not considered adequate, this tough hitch will do the job. If all else fails, it can be used to attach the main sheet tackle to a boom – on a dinghy at least – and then withstand a hard beat into wind and tide to get back to land.

Method: Begin as if to tie a clove hitch (see p. 45) or ground-line hitch (1, and see p. 42), but take the working end around again – first to the right, then to the left, as shown (2). The repetitive wrapping sequence is: over/over/over/over, and finally tuck (3).

Suspend a climbing rope from an overhead tree branch with this knot (but supervise activities for safety).

Lighterman's hitch

Use: When tied around a towing post or hook, this is a superb hitch for securing one boat, barge or ship to another. It also serves to belay a heavy-duty ship's mooring or a marquee guy-line. It holds fast, cannot jam and is quickly cast off.

Use this knot on the guy-lines of tents or awnings.

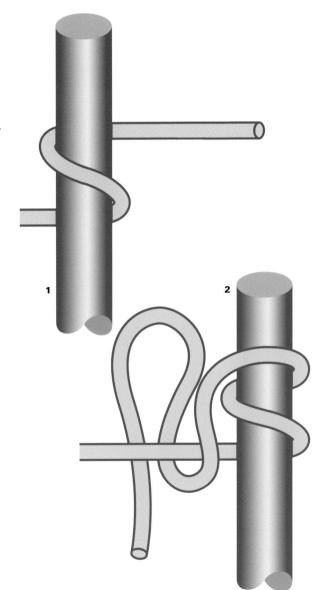

1

2

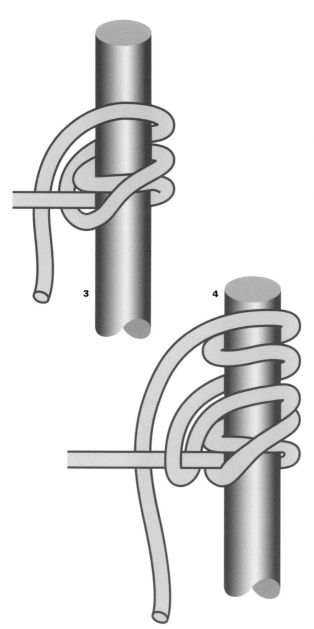

Method: Take a turn (or two or three) to apply whatever friction the job demands (1). Once the strain is taken up and the line length adjusted for the job in hand, take a bight beneath the standing part and hitch it over the post, bollard or stake (2–3). Wrap the end around once or twice and let it hang (4).

51

Pile hitch

Use: This hitch is used for making a line fast to a stake, post, pile or bollard. It is best tied in the bight.

Method: Take a turn with a bight beneath the standing part and place it over the post (1–3).

If a strong dog insists on pulling, wrap the loop of its lead around your wrist in this way.

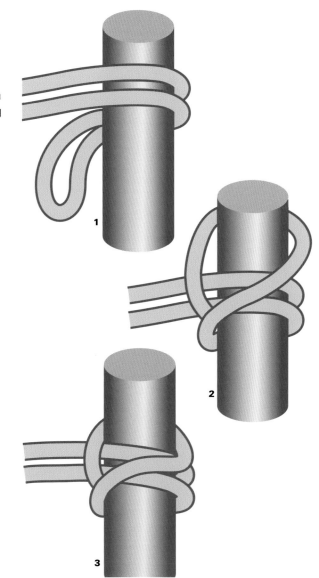

52

World's fair knot

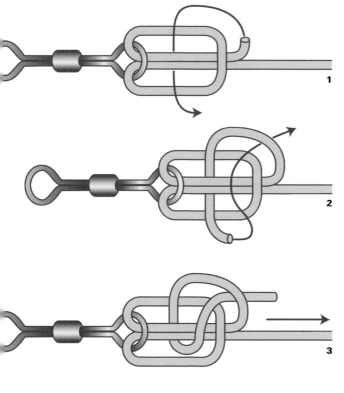

1

2

3

Use: This relatively new knot secures line to hook to other terminal tackle by means of a loop or long bight of doubled line, but, unlike the Palomar knot (see p. 54), would work without a hook or other item of hardware tucked through it.

Method: Pass a loop through the ring or eye and double it over to lay upon both standing parts. Take the working end and make a locking tuck, going over/under(two parts)/over (1), then tuck the tag end back through the loop created in step 1 (2). Pull the tag end and standing part in opposite directions to realign the knot and tighten it (3–4).

4

This knot is best used to attach fishing line to hooks.

As with all angling knots, this knot tends to jam, and must be cut off after use.

Palomar knot

Use: A very strong knot (95–100 per cent) for attaching hooks, swivels, lures or sinkers, or which may be used as an arbor knot to attach monofilament or braid to a reel or spool.

Method: Tie an overhand knot (see p. 12) in the bight, including the ring (or hook, lure or swivel) (1). Then tuck the ring through the loop (2), bring the loop back over the knot to form a collar around the standing part (3) and tighten everything (4).

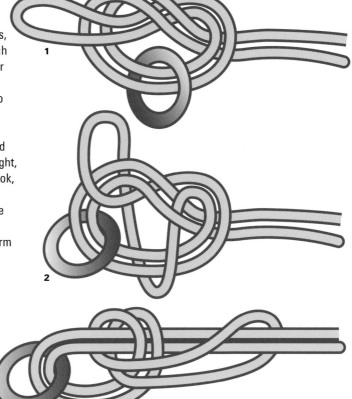

An angling knot to attach hooks and swivels to line.

Jansik special

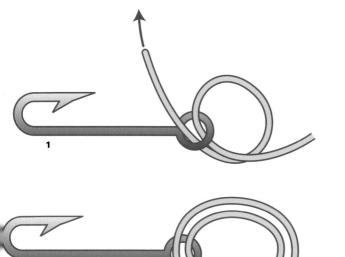

Use: A very strong (98–100 per cent) attachment for a hook, lure or swivel.

Method: Pass the working end twice through the ring (1–2) and then wrap three times through the three adjacent loops of line (3). Moisten the knot and pull steadily on hook, standing part and tag end at once to tighten the knot (4).

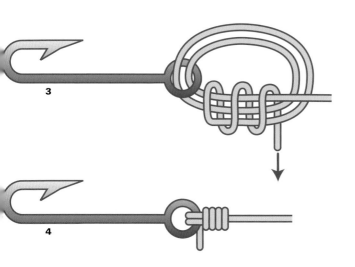

This is the strongest of all the knots for attaching hooks to lines.

Trilene knot

✓ *This knot is best used to attach line to a hook with an eye.*

Use: Hook knots are stronger when the line has been passed twice through the eye of the hook, where the size of both eye and line allow the modification. This is one of several such knots. It can be troublesome to tighten in lines over about 5.5 kg (12 lb) breaking strength. Still, it is a popular knot.

Method: Take a round turn (see p. 46) through the eye or ring and then wrap the working end four or five times around the standing part of the line. Bring the end back and tuck it through the round turn (1). Pull, push and generally knead the knot into a blood knot form before tightening it (2–3).

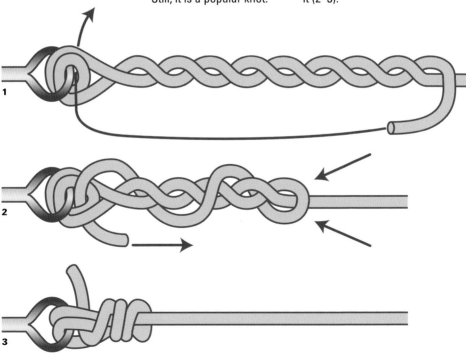

1

2

3

Domhof knot

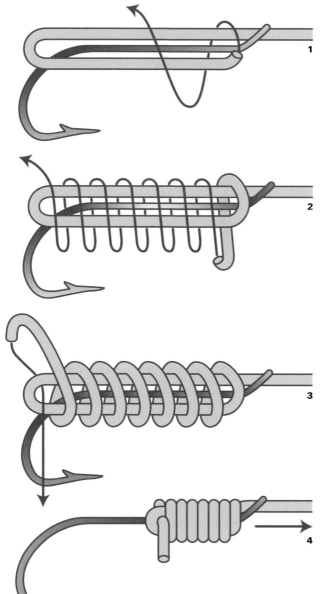

Use: This is one of a group of knots known collectively as trombone knots – the knot is tightened by pulling on the standing part so the excess loop disappears like the slide on a trombone.

Method: Pass the end of a line through an angled (up or down) hook eye and bring it back to create a trombone loop (1). Enclose both loop legs together with the hook shank in a series of neatly bedded wrapping turns (2). Finally tuck the end through what remains of the loop (3) and pull upon the standing part of the line to tighten the knot and trap the tag end (4).

This knot can be used to make a decorative pull for a window blind. ✔

57

Prusik knot

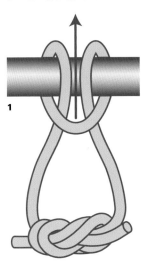

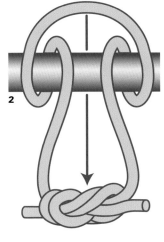

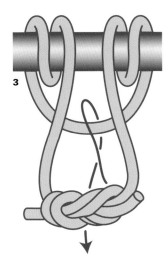

 A useful safety mechanism for climbers and cavers.

Use: This is a slide-and-grip hitch, recommended for climbers faced with an emergency ascent, such as getting out of a cave or crevasse. It works in the following way. The climber attaches two endless slings or strops to the main climbing rope with prusik knots. Both slings pass through his chest harness and he stands in the lower one and slides up the hitch of the other. He then transfers his weight into the raised sling and repeats the process with the lower one. By this alternate load – unload – move process, a virtual rope ladder is created – it's the nearest thing to hauling yourself up by your own bootstraps. Experts have been timed climbing 30 metres (100 ft) in just over one minute, or 120 metres (400 ft) in a little over nine minutes.

There are now several prusik knots or hitches, varying in reliability and ease of use. None of them, however, can be easily released while jammed and fully loaded; weight must first be taken off the knot and the turns worked loose. Both hands may be needed; be warned that careless use among climbers has caused many accidents and even the occasional fatality. A karabiner may be inserted to ease movement of the knots, although the climber must still be clipped in to the bights of the slings. The prusik may be used in abseiling or rappelling, but climbers must make sure that the knots are within reach and will not leave them hanging helplessly if they lose control.

Method: Use 7-mm (¼-in) accessory cord; thinner stuff will be weaker, and anything thicker will not grip as well. The cord should not be more than half the diameter of the main rope. Allow enough length, as each knot may use at least 60 cm (2 ft) of line, and the slings should be the right length for you to reach the knots comfortably.

Experts disagree over whether or not there is any advantage to be gained from using rope and slings of similar composition. Softer laid or braided (i.e., more flexible) slings will grip the rope well but will be difficult to loosen and shift; while harder laid or braided cord may be more prone to slipping. Do not use tape, for which there are other more suitable friction hitches.

A properly tied prusik knot should be able to hold until the sling cord breaks. If it begins to slip under load, it may continue to do so until the heat generated melts the nylon knot and it comes completely undone (quite apart from any damage done to the main climbing rope).

Loop the sling round the main line, and lead it through (1). Take the loop of the hitch round the main line (2). Then lead the sling through the loop (3) to make a double wrap (4). To prevent the knot sliding – especially in icy or muddy conditions – the basic two-wrap knot (2) may have to be increased to three (5), a double prusik knot, or even four wrapping turns.

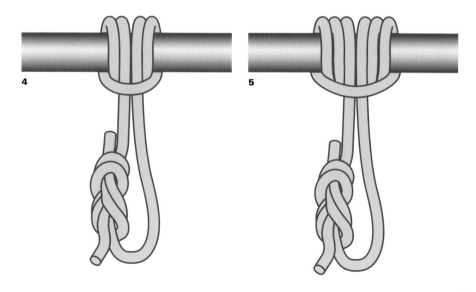

4

5

Extended French prusik knot

 Use in place of a bracket, ring or other anchorage point.

Use: This innovative friction hitch absorbs the energy of a shock loading by sliding; it does not grip firmly until the falling load is low enough. The knot exerts friction on the enclosed rope by stretching and decreasing its diameter, so applying inward pressure and spreading the friction over a wide area.

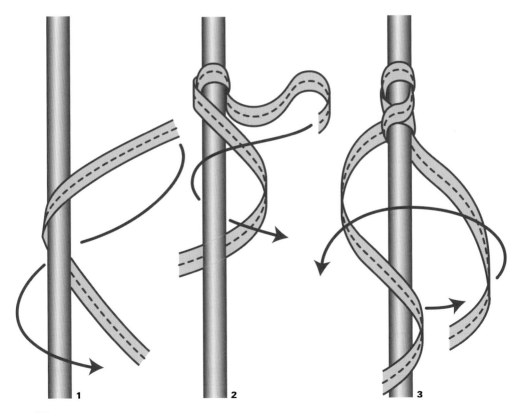

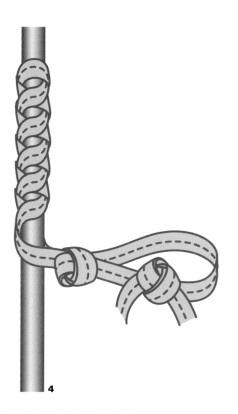

4

5

Method: At first sight this knot looks complex, but it becomes easy with practice. Use 25-mm (1-in) tape. (Tubular tape is probably best.) Eight to ten racking turns are sufficient (1–3). The cross-overs must alternate, and the window spaces must be as small as possible (i.e., only a little of the rope should be visible). Join the two ends as close to the knot as possible, the tighter the better (4). (5) shows another method using pre-tied loops.

Illustrated here on a single rope, the French prusik knot works equally well on doubled abseil or rappel lines. To release it, grasp the upper part of the knot and tug it down to shorten the knot.

Cat's paw

Use: This strong ring hitch attaches the loop of a Bimini twist (see pp. 88–9) or other similar long loop to a swivel or a hook, primarily for offshore big-game fishing.

Method: Pass the end of a loop through ring or eye and double it back on itself (1). Next tuck the hook or swivel, in a succession of backward somersaults (a total of seven to ten), through the space between the inert loop legs and the loop itself (2). There should then be an identical number of twists on each side of the knot, one set spiralling left-handed or clockwise, the others right-handed or anti-clockwise (counterclockwise). Pull on both loop legs, straightening them (3), and then slide the wrapping turns that result close together alongside the point of attachment (4).

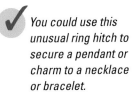

You could use this unusual ring hitch to secure a pendant or charm to a necklace or bracelet.

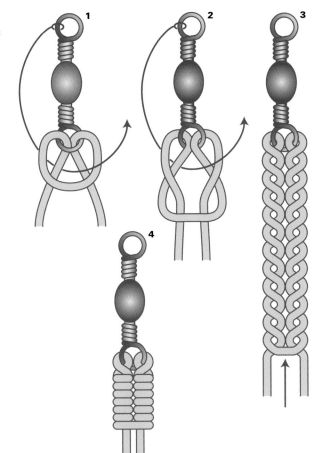

loops

Fixed loops are often used as temporary hitches, to tie up a boat or ship, because they can be cast off and reused without the need to untie and retie them. They are also used to begin parcel ties and other lashings or seizings. Anglers use loops for the start of any tackle system, while climbers employ them as life-support or rescue knots.

Sliding loops – commonly referred to as nooses – must be used more selectively, as they will tighten when loaded, but may not readily slacken off again. Nooses that can be easily adjusted for size by hand, but which then lock up when loaded, make useful guy-lines for tents, flag poles and radio masts. They will also tension a washing line.

The Bowline is the King of Knots because it is strong, secure, and versatile, as kings should be. And simple, as kings generally are '

Brian Toss, *The Rigger's Apprentice,* **1984**

loops

Double overhand loop knot

Use: This is a fairly strong and secure loop for slick modern materials.

Method: Make a longish bight in the end of the line and tie the doubled line into a simple overhand knot (1, and see p. 12). Tuck the bight a second time to end up with a double overhand knot (2). Tighten the knot slowly and carefully, kneading it into the form of a blood knot (3, and see pp. 34–35), at the same time keeping the knot parts parallel to eliminate lumpy distortion of the completed knot. Then finish tightening it (4).

 A very stong knot which works well when tied in nylon fishing line.

1

2

3

4

Triple overhand loop knot

Use: This is a chunkier and stronger version of the preceding knot. Even more turns may be added, when it will do instead of a Bimini twist (see pp. 88–89). The extra tuck(s) would not have been required in the days of gut and horsehair. But lines are now slicker and so increased friction is demanded from the knots used in them. A multiple overhand loop is widely known as the surgeon's loop, but the angling application is also called the thumb loop, spider knot or loop and sometimes (quite wrongly) spider hitch.

Method: Make a long bight in the end of the line and tie a double overhand knot (1, and see p. 12). Add a third tuck to make a triple overhand knot (2) and begin the tightening process that will convert it into a blood knot (see pp. 34–35), taking care to remove unwanted twists in the doubled lines. Finally tighten the knot (3). It is claimed by some that this knot is easier to tie than a Bimini twist (see pp. 88–89) – and it certainly requires less effort – but it can easily be botched and emerge as a bird's nest of tangled coils.

This knot can be used to rig a weaving loom.

It should not be used on coarse cordage.

Scaffold knot

Use: This tough noose knot can endure repeated use due to the insertion of a plastic or metal lining called a thimble. Sailors refer to this as a 'hard eye' Thimbles come in a range of sizes and are obtainable from boat and yacht chandlers.

Method: First make the loop and tighten the sliding knot (1–3). Next, insert the thimble (4). See that its jaws bed down into the throat of the noose and pull the whole lot snug. To attach a line directly to a ring or bracket, without using a shackle, fix the thimble in place and pass the working end of the line around it before tying.

 Inserting a thimble inside this loop will protect against wear from chafing.

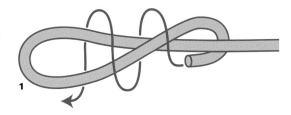

1

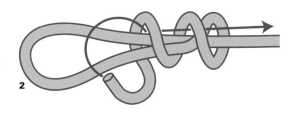

2

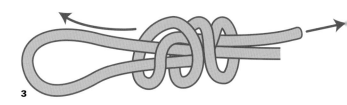

3

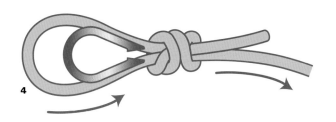

4

Bowline in the bight

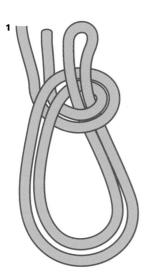

1

Use: There are tested and certificated ladders and harnesses for the well-prepared, but all sailors sooner or later are faced with some urgent improvisation. This can be used for lowering an injured person. One leg is put through each loop and the patient (if conscious and capable) holds tight onto the rope at chest level, or is somehow secured to it. It reduces the strength of the line in which it is tied by up to 40 per cent.

Method: As this knot is usually tied in the middle of a rope, it must be made without using either end. Make a long bight and begin with the doubled rope as if tying an orthodox bowline ((1), and see pp. 68–69). Bend the single working bight down, lift the two larger standing loops up through it (2), and allow the single bight to go back up again. The completed knot will be doubled throughout, except for the single bight around the standing parts (3).

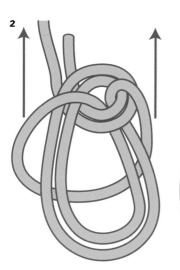

2

3

Climbers can use this knot to spread the load between two anchorage points.

Bowline

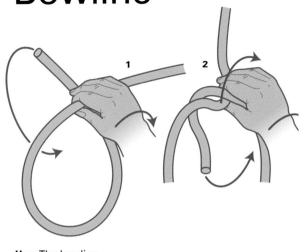

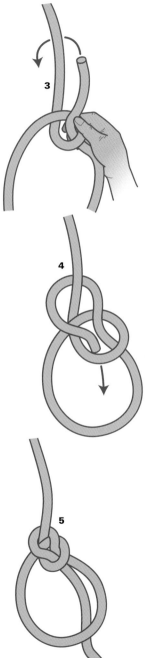

Use: The bowline (pronounced 'boh-linn') makes a fixed loop. It reduces the breaking strength of any stuff in which it is tied by as much as 40 per cent. Nevertheless the bowline can be used for a wide range of jobs, from securing the string before tying a parcel, to outdoor pursuits such as climbing.

 Cast a bowline over a bollard to 'hang off' a boat mooring.

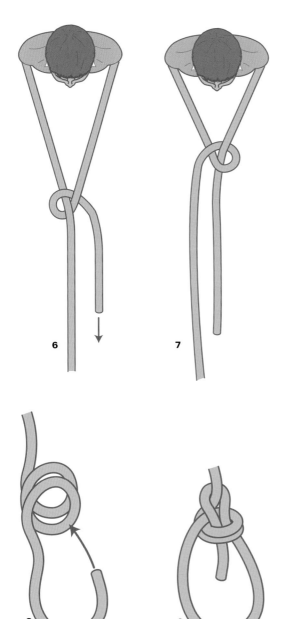

Method: Once learnt, this knot can be formed with a fluent, one-handed twist of the wrist (1–5). You should also work out how to tie a bowline viewed from an unfamiliar angle (6–7). Imagine facing someone, passing a rope around behind them, beneath their armpits, then having to make the knot. The trick is to first take a turn around the standing part of the rope with your working end. Next, pull it out straight to transfer the underhand loop in the standing part. Finally, pass and tuck the working end to lock off in the usual way.

If the knot will have to withstand rough treatment, tie the double bowline (8–9). This has a breaking strength of 70–75 per cent and is therefore stronger and far more secure than a basic bowline.

Triple bowline

Use: Generally, I do not recommend any ad hoc rope slings and chairs for working aloft or over the side, but that said, the triple bowline can be used to make an emergency sit sling, chest sling or full harness. The loops must be painstakingly adjusted to fit the appropriate parts of the body.

Method: Tie an otherwise orthodox bowline (see pp. 68–69) in a doubled bight of rope (1–4). Adjusting the first two loops and accommodating the slack in the final one is fiddly to do but not too hard to figure out.

 This knot can be used to make an emergency sling or harness.

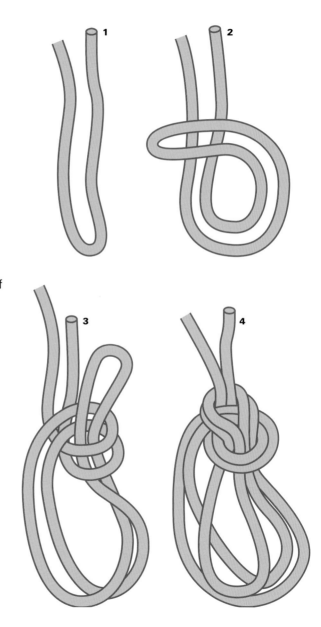

Triple bowline variation

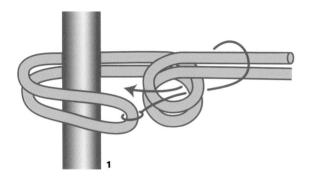

Use: This variation is useful for training purposes, when it can be used for belaying to a fixed anchorage (e.g., a tree). It has a loop plus two lines to which an instructor and pupil can be attached.

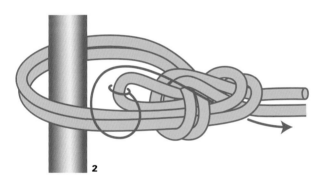

Method: Tie a triple bowline (see opposite) in the doubled rope (1–2) and tuck the working bight back through to create a figure eight layout in the completed knot (3).

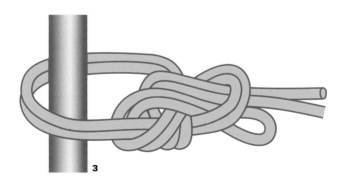

A useful knot for supporting multiple loads.

Angler's loop knot

Use: This knot makes a relatively strong and very secure fixed loop in anything from slender monofilament to large rope.

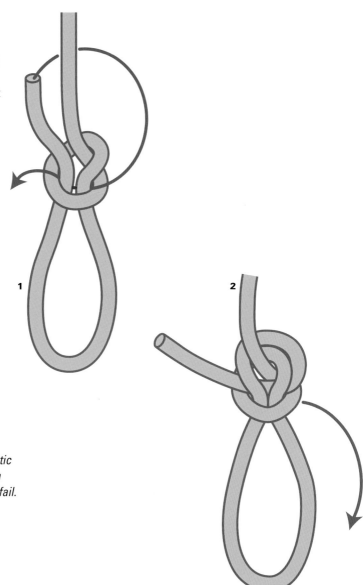

1

2

✓ *This knot suits synthetic lines and works when other loop knots may fail.*

Rear view

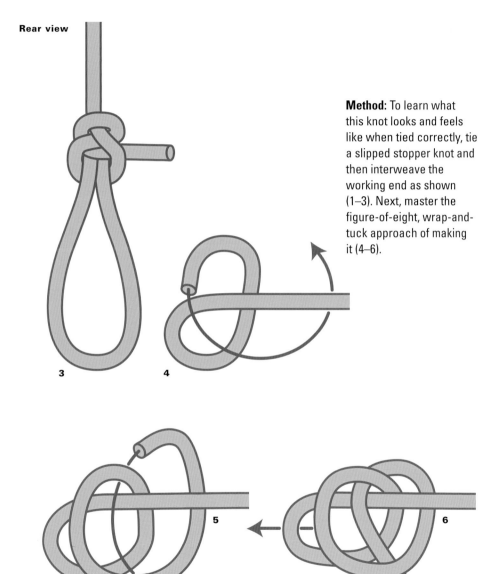

Method: To learn what this knot looks and feels like when tied correctly, tie a slipped stopper knot and then interweave the working end as shown (1–3). Next, master the figure-of-eight, wrap-and-tuck approach of making it (4–6).

3

4

5

6

Alpine butterfly

Use: This is a fixed loop tied in the bight of a rope and the middle climber of a team of three clips into it. It can be pulled in two (or even three) directions at once without distorting or capsizing. It can also be used as a temporary means of using a damaged rope, by isolating a flawed section within the loop.

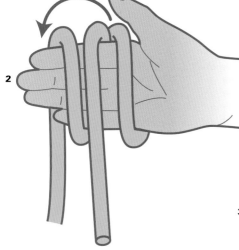

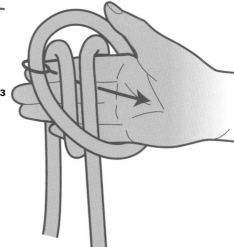

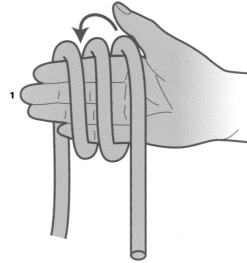

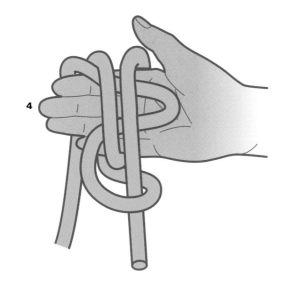

4

Method: There are several ways of tying this knot and you must seek the guidance of experienced climbers whichever you use. The method shown here is possibly the easiest to learn. Take two round turns and transfer the right-hand part to the middle (1). Transfer the new right-hand part across to the extreme left-hand side (2) and then pull a bight through beneath the two remaining knot parts (3–4). The resulting loop knot is symmetrical (5). Work it snug and tight (6).

5

This knot can be used to repair a damaged rope.

6

75

Frost knot

Use: This knot is used to make the steps or rungs in the short, improvised webbing or tape ladders known as *étriers*.

Primarily a climber's device, this is the only effective way to tie loops in flat woven tape, webbing lashings or slings.

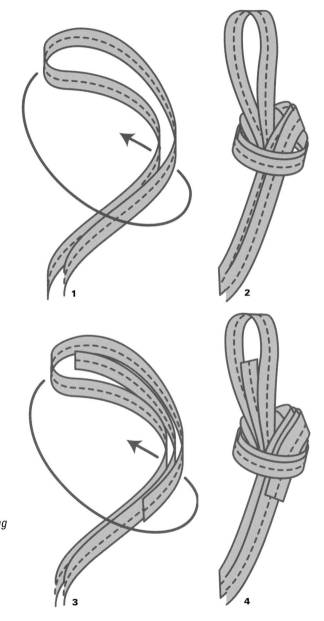

5

Method: This is like an overhand loop knot (1–2), and see p. 64 (1) but incorporates both webbing parts and ends in the completed knot (3–4). Like the double Frost knot (5–7), it is related to the tape knot (see pp. 22–23).

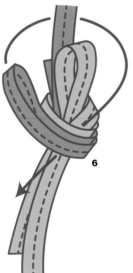

6

7

Midshipman's hitch

Use: Primarily an adjustable loop for moorings, guy-lines, etc., the midshipman's hitch has even been suggested (minus the final half-hitch) as a quick way to attach yourself to a life-line in an emergency. In a situation of this kind, grip the working end to the standing part with at least one hand.

Method: Make a loop on the rope (1), and take two adjacent diagonal turns on the side of the knot from which the pull will come (2). Lead the working end around the standing part and back through on itself (3). Adjust to tighten (4).

 Useful for suspending hanging indoor plants, as the height can be easily adjusted.

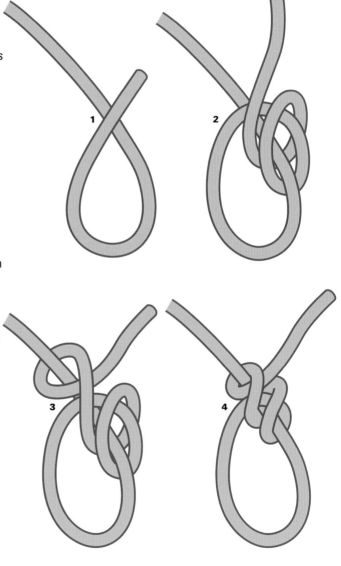

Tarbuck knot

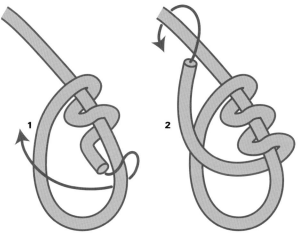

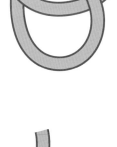

Use: A useful all-purpose slide-and-grip loop.

Work the entire knot snug before use. The knot relies for its grip on creating a dog's-leg kink in its own standing part (4). This is impossible if the line is tied to a separate and unyielding foundation.

Method: Take two and a half turns with the working end around the standing part, bringing it out through the loop so formed (1–2). Then twist the working end in a figure eight around the standing part and under itself, as shown (3).

Use this knot to moor small craft temporarily on a rising or falling tide.

Do not use on synthetic sheath and core (kernmantel) climbing ropes.

Figure eight loops

Use: The figure eight knot layout is a versatile alternative to a bowline, a bowline in the bight or a triple bowline (see pp. 68, 67 and 70) for tying into the rope, anchoring non-climbers, or any other purpose for which a single, double or triple loop knot is required.

 Climbers prefer these knots as they are easily learned and recalled, even in difficult conditions.

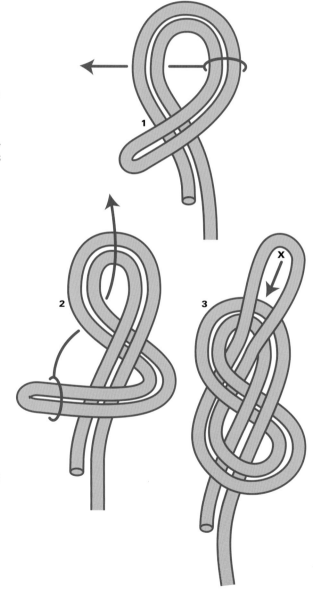

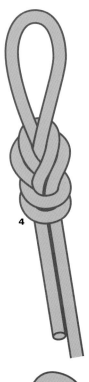

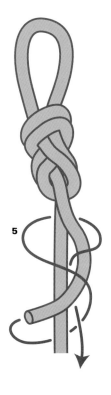

Method: Tie directly in the bight (1–4) to form a single loop knot. Remove any twists so that paired parts of the knot are parallel with one another. To ensure maximum strength, climbers recommend that the standing bight – marked X in 3 – should lie on the outside of the bend, with the working-end bight on the inside. Secure the working end with an overhand knot to the standing part (5–6), or tuck it back through the knot (7). This knot uses 1.2 metres (4 ft) of 9-mm (³⁄₁₀-in) rope and 1.5 metres (5 ft) of 11-mm (⅜-in) rope.

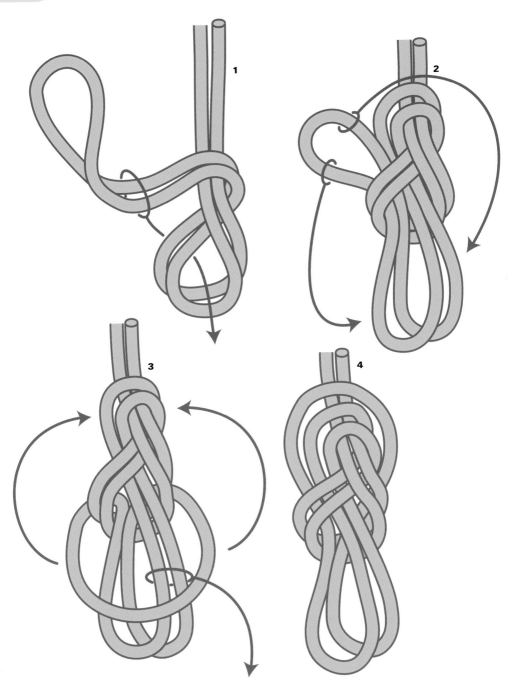

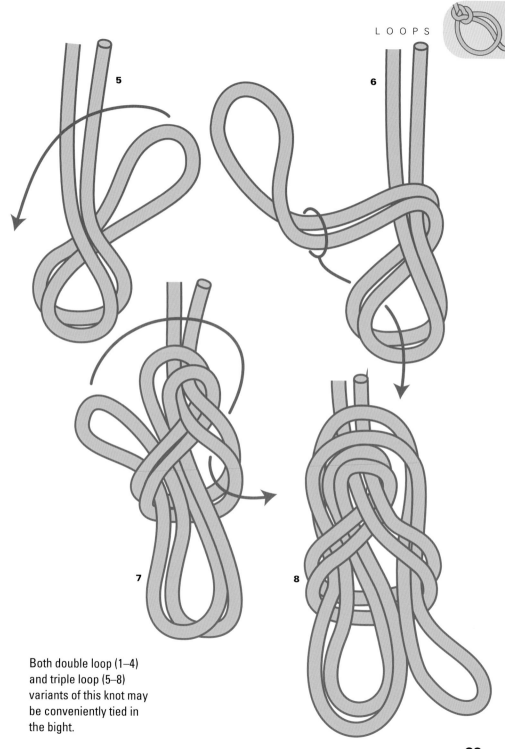

Both double loop (1–4)
and triple loop (5–8)
variants of this knot may
be conveniently tied in
the bight.

Rapala knot

Use: This knot makes a small fixed loop that allows a fishing lure to move realistically. It is recommended for plugs, but it will suit any sort of lure or fly that needs freedom to wriggle or wobble about enticingly.

Method: Tie a simple overhand or thumb knot before passing the working end through the ring or other attachment. Tuck the end back through the initial knot in the opposite direction, creating a skewed slip knot, and adjust the loop to the required size (1). Wrap and tuck the end as shown (2–4). Work everything tight and snug (5).

This fishing knot was specifically designed for use with plugs.

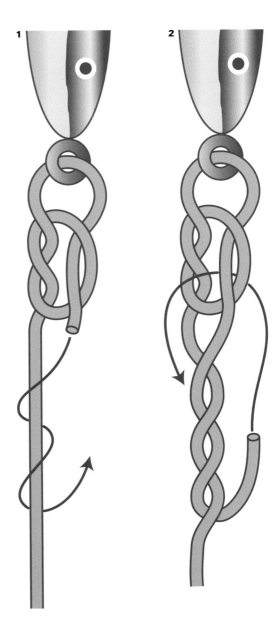

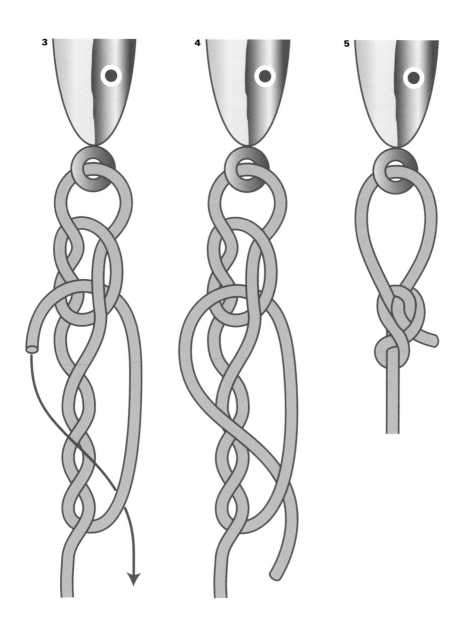

Blood knot loop

Use: Use this to create a loop in a thinner line, which is then attached to a thicker backing line.

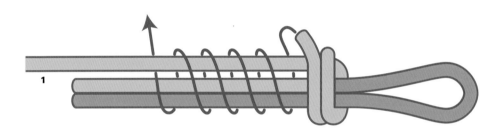

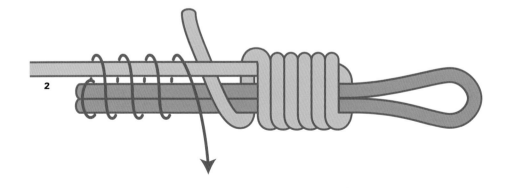

Method: Double or middle a length of line to make a bight and wrap the working end of another line around both legs of the initial bight at least three times before tucking it (1). Then wrap and tuck the twin ends of the loop line to complete this compound knot (2). Pull it tight (3).

3

Can be used to join lines of different size.

Bimini twist

Use: This – like the plaited or braided loop (see pp. 90–91) – is claimed to be as strong (100 per cent) as an unknotted fishing line and is recommended for the same uses. It lacks the in-built stretchiness of the plait under load.

 This is the strongest knot for big-game fishing.

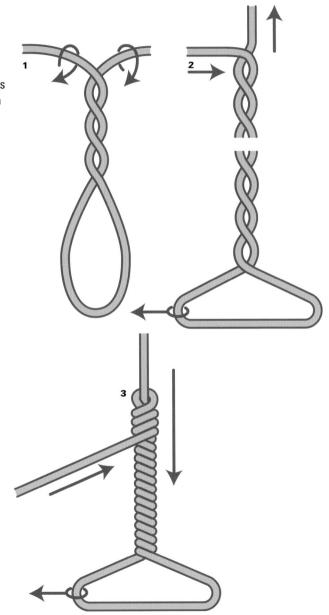

Method: Double the line into a bight that is at least 1 m (3 ft) long and twist 20 or so turns into it (1). Pull the loop outwards forcibly to compress the initial twists, with your feet or knees, or get someone else to help (2). Hold the standing part of the line firmly in one hand, and use the fingers of your other hand to pull the working end out at right-angles to it, and as the loop is forced open counter-turns will be created at the upper end of the twists (3).

Feed the accumulating secondary layer of wrapping turns neatly downwards towards the loop. Finish off the knot in one of two ways. Either add a couple of half hitches (4) or apply at least five or six seizing turns over a doubled back tag end (5) which must then be pulled tight (6).

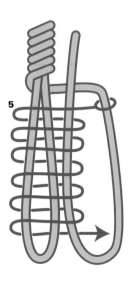

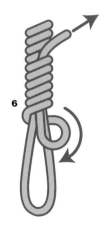

Plaited or braided loop

Use: This is claimed to be one of the strongest of all loops (100 per cent – that is, as strong as the unknotted line) and is recommended for the start of any tackle system intended for deep-sea, blue-water big game fishing.

This extraordinary loop has an inherent stretch that makes it suitable for use when an abrupt shock loading may be incurred.

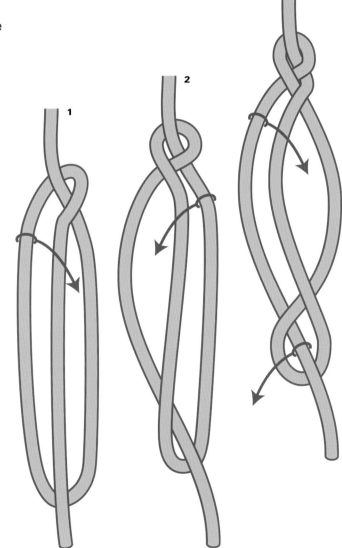

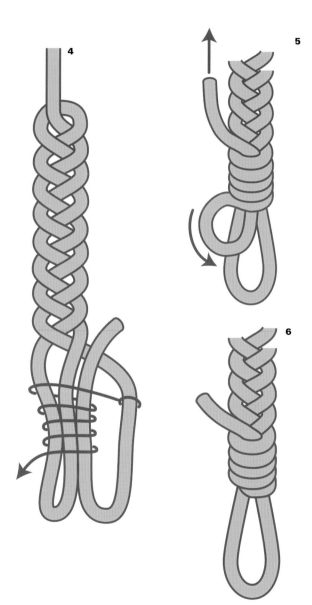

Method: Lay out the line as shown (1) and bring the left-hand part of it over (in front) to become the new centre strand. Next bring the right-hand strand over to become the centre strand (2). Then bring the left-hand strand over to become the centre strand (3). Repeat (2) and (3) to creat a three-strand pigtail plait or braid. The loosely woven mirror image of this plait will become tangled lower down in the long bight, so pull out the standing end periodically to untangle it. When several centimetres (inches) of plait have been made, turn what has so far been the working end back on itself and then take at least four or five wrapping turns with the same strand around both loop legs and its own end (4). Close up the smaller loop created by pulling on the tag end (5), fully tightening the whipping to complete this loop knot (6).

Adjustable loop and bend

Use: This practical slide-and-grip knot can be grasped and shifted easily by hand in either direction but locks up firmly under load. After the load is removed, the knot may be slid along the rope again. The momentum of a fall will cause the knot to slide and so absorb energy. The slippage load is predictable and can be controlled to some extent – any variation will be the result of inconsistent tying.

Method: Use rope or webbing (tape). Take two turns round the standing part, then once round the resulting loop, tucking the working end back under itself (1). The tape ends should be left at least 8 cm (3 in) long. For real peace of mind, add an overhand knot (see page 12) to each end, or turn the ends back on themselves and sew them in place to form bulky tabs.

Two of these knots can be tied together to form an endless sling (2–3). If the two knots are kept apart, then each is able to act as its own Prusik (see pp. 58–59) – should one knot fail, the second serves as a back-up; if both slip, they merely come together and hold like a fisherman's knot (see p. 27).

1

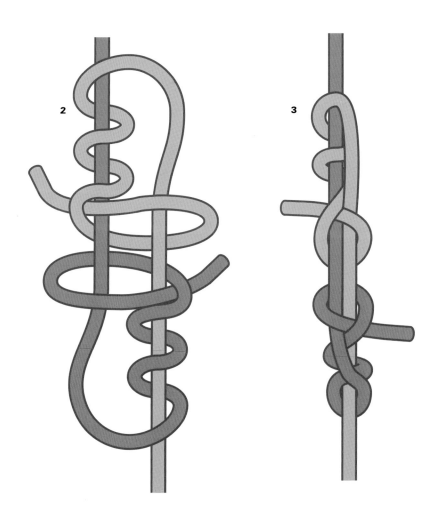

A slide-and-grip shock-absorbing knot designed for climbers.

Glossary

A

Abseil To descend an anchored climbing rope in a controlled way (also known as rappelling)

Anchor An attachment for securing vessels on sea or river bed; a safety device for climbers (*see* Belay)

Arbor The axle, spindle or middle of a reel spool, to which fishing line is attached

B

Barrel knot *See* Blood knot

Belay To secure or anchor a climbing position with ropes and fixings

Bend The generic name for the many knots that join two separate ropes

Bight An acute bend or partial loop in a rope

Binding knot Knots useful for tying up bundles, sails, kitbags or unwieldy loads such as oars

Blood knot Any one of a group of strong and secure barrel-shaped knots, with characteristic wrapping turns, particularly favoured by anglers and climbers

Breaking strength The manufacturer's calculation of the load that will cause a rope to fail, taking no account of any weakening factors

C

Cable A large rope laid up left-handed from three hawser-laid ropes

Capsize (of knots) To become deformed due to incorrect tying or misuse, or in untying

Cord Line under 25-mm (1-in) in circumference or approximately 10-mm (½-in) in diameter (*see* Small stuff)

Cringle An eye at the edge of a sail, formed from a loop or grommet

D

Dog To secure the working end of a rope by wrapping it several times around its own standing part, or another rope

E

Efficiency The strength of any knot, as a percentage of the breaking strength of the rope or cordage in which it is tied

Elbow Two crossing points created close together by a bight

End The working end of a rope or cordage (*see* Standing end)

Eye A loop commonly in the end of a line

F

Fibre The smallest element in vegetable-rope construction, twisted to create yarns

Fid A spike for separating strands of rope when splicing

Flype British dialect word meaning to turn inside out in a smooth peeling action

Fray Deliberate or accidental unlaying of a rope, causing it to be teased out into its component strands and yarns

H

Halyard Line for hoisting or lowering a sail, spar or flag

Hard eye An eye reinforced with a metal or plastic thimble

Hard laid (Of rope and cordage) Highly tensioned during manufacture

Hawser Any three-stranded rope over 25-mm (1-in) in circumference or 10-mm (½-in) in diameter

Hitch The generic name for any knot used to attach a line to a ring, rail, post or line

K

Karabiner A D-shaped or pear-shaped metal snap-ring, with a pivoting gate that can be securely closed; used by climbers

Knot The general name for all rope and cordage entanglements, but specifically one tied in the end of a line, or with both ends of the same line, or in small stuff

L

Lanyard A short length of cord used to lash or secure an item of equipment

Lashing Rope or cord used for binding or securing

Lead (Say 'leed') The direction taken by cordage around or through an object or knot.

Leader A short length of gut, monofilament, braid or wire attaching a fishing hook to a line

Line Any rope with a particular function; e.g., a tow line, clothes-line or mooring line

Loop A bight with a crossing point

Lure An artificial bait

M

Make fast To secure a line to an anchorage or belay

Middle To double a rope or cord prior to use

Monofilament Long synthetic thread made of a single strand

N

Natural fibre Raw material used in vegetable-rope construction

Noose A sliding loop

P

Plug Artificial hooked bait resembling a dead fish that can be made to dart and vibrate

R

Rappel *See* Abseil

Reef To roll up (or fold and tie) sails, reducing their area in strong wind

Rope Any line over 25-mm (1-in) in circumference or about 10-mm (½-in) in diameter; larger than cord

Round turn In which a working end completely encircles a ring, rail, post or another line, and is then brought alongside its own standing part

S

Safe working load The estimated load a rope may safely withstand, taking into account its age, condition and usage; it may be as little as one-sixth of the quoted breaking strength

Security A knot's integral ability to withstand intermittent tugs, shaking, etc.

Seizing Tight binding of thread or cord to grip and hold two ropes, or two parts of the same rope

Sling A knotted or spliced endless band or strop

Small stuff A casual and imprecise term for any cordage (as opposed to rope)

Snell A whipping or binding that secures line to the straight shank of a hook, especially an eyeless (spade-ended) one

Snub Stop or check the motion of a boat by taking turns of a rope around a post, bollard or other fixed object

Soft laid (Of rope and cordage) Flexible due to the absence of tension in manufacture

Standing end The opposite end from the working end

Stanchion Vertical pole or beam used as a support

Standing part That part of rope and cordage between the working and standing ends

Stopper knot A knot used to prevent rope fraying or slipping through a hole

Strength A knot's integral ability to withstand a load

String Domestic-quality small cord or twine

Strop *See* Sling

Synthetic rope Rope and cordage made from monofilaments

T

Tag end An angling term for the working end of a line

Tape Flat or tubular woven nylon or polyester webbing used instead of cordage for some knotting applications

Thimble A metal or plastic reinforcement for seized or spliced eyes; used in sailing

Thread Fine line

Turn A 360-degree wrap around a ring, rail, post or rope

W

Whipping A method of binding a rope's end to prevent fraying

Working end The end of rope or cord that is available for use

Index and acknowledgements

We would like to thank the following publishers for kindly allowing us to feature quotes from their publications:

The Ivy Press Ltd, Old Candlemakers, West St, Lewes, East Sussex, BN7 2NZ (John Shaw, *The Directory of Knots*, 2003)

International Marine/Ragged Mountain Press, P.O. Box 220/Mail, Camden, ME 04843-0220, 633 Route 1, Rockport, ME 0856, USA (Brian Toss, *The Rigger's Apprentice*, 1984)

Stackpole Books, 5067 Ritter Road, Mechanicsburg, PA 17055-6921, USA (Duane Raleigh, *Knots for Ropes and Climbers*, 1998)

The Rams Skull Press, 12 Fairyland Road, Kuranda, Q4872, Australia (Ron Edwards, *Knots for Horse-lovers*, 2001)

Executive Editor Sarah Tomley
Editor Charlotte Wilson
Executive Art Editor Peter Burt
Designer Ginny Zeal
Production Controller Manjit Sihra
Indexing Indexing Specialists (UK) Ltd